ARTS AND ENTERTAINMENT

Photo credits:

Mike Powell/Allsport: Page 16
Todd Warshaw/Allsport: Page 16
Allsport: Page 17
AP/Wide World Photo: Pages 8, 14, 18
Michael Barson/Archive Photos: Page 10
CBS Photo Archive/Archive Photos: Page 19
Jeff Christensen/Archive Photos: Page 13
Express News/Archive Photos: Page 17
Museum of the City of New York/Archive Photos: Page 13
John Phillip Sousa/Archive Photos: Page 18
Archive Photos: Pages 10, 22, 23, 26, 27
UPI/Corbis-Bettmann: Pages 10, 11
Corbis-Bettmann: Page 12
Porter Gifford/Gamma-Liaison: Pages 28-29; endpages
Armen Kachaturian/Gamma-Liaison: Page 11
Scott McKiernan/Gamma-Liaison: Cover; Page 25
Anthony Suau/Gamma-Liaison: Page 21
Gamma-Liaison: Pages 21, 28
Kwame Brathwaite/Globe Photo: Page 15
Harvey Caufman/Globe Photo: Page 17
NBC/Globe Photo: Page 22
Globe Photo: Pages 6-7, 11, 12, 19, 24, 29
The Granger Collection: Pages 6, 8, 10, 18, 19
Hulton Getty Images: Pages 7, 8, 12
Michael J. Howell/International Stock: Page 9
David Norton/International Stock: Pages 12-13
International Stock: Pages 8, 9
The Kobal Collection: Cover; Pages: 7, 14, 15, 23, 26, 27, 28, 29
Jay Blakesberg/Retna: Pages 20-21
Andrew Kent/Retna: Pages 20, 28
Frank Micelotta/Retna: Page 20
Doc Pele/Stills/Retna: Cover; Page 20
Stills/Retna: Page 14
Retna: Page 15
Children's Television Workshop/Shooting Star: Page 25
Embassy Films/Shooting Star: Page 13
Yoram Kahana/Shooting Star: Page 23
S.S. Archives/Shooting Star: Pages 22, 26
Bruce W. Talamon/Shooting Star: Page 21
Walt Disney Productions/Shooting Star: Page 22

Visit us at www.kidsbooks.com
Volume discounts available for group purchases.

EYES ON AMERICA™

ARTS AND ENTERTAINMENT

Written by
Celia Bland

kidsbooks®
Incorporated

THE AMERICAN STORY

Everybody loves a good story. Probably as old as the campfire itself, stories are the basis for much art and entertainment. Whether they're based in fact or entirely made-up, or told through print, radio, TV, or film, American stories have something important to tell about the nation itself.

◀ POETRY IN MOTION

"Listen my children, and you shall hear, of the midnight ride of Paul Revere." So wrote Henry Wadsworth Longfellow. This world-famous poet told stories about real Americans: pilgrims (Miles Standish), Native American chiefs (Hiawatha), and patriots of the American Revolution.

TOO TALL TO BELIEVE ▲

Exaggerated stories known as tall tales were created in America by loggers, cattle drivers, railroad workers, and slaves. According to one tale, John Henry, a freed slave, stood taller than a tree, could eat 20 chickens at a sitting, and could swing two 20-pound hammers, driving steel spikes into railroad ties faster than anyone alive.

◀ NATIONAL WIT

In the 1800s, when you heard "Mark twain!" shouted on the Mississippi River, it meant the water was 12 feet deep and safe for steamboats. Today, Mark Twain is better known as the pen name of Samuel Clemens, author of *Tom Sawyer* and *Huckleberry Finn*. An American humorist, Twain traveled around the world, telling stories and trying to get people to laugh at their own shortcomings.

In the movie *Independence Day*, aliens continue to capture the imagination of America, especially when they're attacking a national institution.

ALIEN RADIO

On the night of October 30, 1938, radio listeners were stunned by a news flash: aliens from Mars had landed in New Jersey! This landmark broadcast, a clever reworking of H. G. Wells's sci-fi novel *The War of the Worlds*, brought hysteria to listeners and fame to the show's creator, Orson Welles.

ROOTS OF TV ▲

Roots began as a Pulitzer Prize-winning novel in which author Alex Haley told the story of his family, from their African origins through slavery to freedom after the Civil War. The novel, published in 1976, was adapted into a 12-hour television miniseries, which aired in 1977 to a record 80 million viewers.

CLIFFHANGERS

From their beginnings in the early 1900s, movies have been an excellent way to tell stories. One of the first "chapter stories" was *The Perils of Pauline* series. These short suspenseful films always left the heroine (played by Pearl White) in a dangerous situation—often tied to railroad tracks with a train approaching!

CROWD PLEASERS

Americans love the excitement of large-scale public entertainment—from parades and light shows to the circus and theme parks. In America, if you build it or stage it, the public will come!

WESTWARD HO!

"Buffalo Bill" Cody's "Wild West Show" thrilled and chilled 19th-century audiences with simulated stagecoach hold-ups, a re-creation of Custer's Last Stand, trick and pony-express riders, and Cody's star cowgirl, Calamity Jane.

ONE-MAN SHOW

A master of sleight-of-hand tricks, Harry Houdini (1874-1926) was world famous for his sensational escapes from police handcuffs, straitjackets, and prison cells. One time, Houdini had himself tied, locked into a case, which was then bound with steel bands, and thrown into New York's harbor. Houdini appeared on the surface just 59 seconds later.

CIRCUS! CIRCUS!

When the Ringling Brothers took over the Barnum & Bailey Circus in 1907, *The Greatest Show on Earth* opened. Featuring Jumbo the six-ton elephant, the show traveled with its own power plant to generate electricity for 300 tents. Today, more than 40 circus companies tour the U.S. each year.

Every July 4th, Americans celebrate the signing of the Declaration of Independence with huge, public fireworks displays.

ON PARADE ▲

Whether completely serious or all for fun, a parade is intended to draw a crowd. Perhaps nowhere is there a parade more spectacular than the one sponsored by Macy's department store and staged in New York City on Thanksgiving Day. Held every year since 1924, the parade features celebrities, elaborate floats, marching bands, and gigantic balloons.

A magical tunnel of glowing neon lights welcomes people to EPCOT in Orlando, Florida.

FUN PARKS

In the early 1950s, Walt Disney bought 182 acres of orange grove in California. His vision: a theme park of rides and entertainments for the whole family. He called this "magic kingdom" Disneyland. Walt Disney World, in Florida, soon followed, featuring a theme park, hotels, and a city of the future: The Environmental Prototype of the City of Tomorrow (EPCOT).

THE AMERICAN LOOK

American artists, long under the shadow of European styles and traditions, have always tried to find a new way of seeing— and doing—art.

Crazy Horse Memorial (below) stands 563-feet high—which makes it the biggest sculpture in the whole world!

SHARK ATTACK!
John Singleton Copley's *Watson and the Shark* illustrates a horrific shark attack in 1778. Watson, the young sailor in the water, not only survived (losing a leg to the Great White)— he commissioned the painting!

PORTRAITS OF WAR
Mathew Brady (*right*) was a successful society photographer before he followed the Union Army to the battlefields of the Civil War. His photographs of military leaders, foot soldiers, and the deadly aftermath of battle recorded the devastation of the war.

THE FUNNY PAPERS
Comic strips were invented in the U.S., when on May 5, 1895, Richard Outcault published a political cartoon in the *New York World*—and sales of the newspaper jumped! A comic-strip hero created in 1938, *Superman* was lifted off the page to become the star of a radio series, movie serials, a television series, and feature films.

SUPERMAN

64 PAGES OF ACTION!

ALL IN FULL COLOR

THE COMPLETE STORY OF THE DARING EXPLOITS OF THE ONE AND ONLY SUPERMAN

POP ART

In 1962, Andy Warhol (1928-1987) exhibited his first silk-screened paintings of Campbell's soup cans as Pop Art—art that was meant to comment on, illustrate, and manipulate society. He favored the techniques of commercial art, printing series of photo-graphic images in garish colors.

IT'S NEVER TOO LATE ▼

Anna Mary Robertson (1860-1961), known as Grandma Moses, spent most of her life doing farm work. Then, at age 78, her hands virtually crippled with arthritis, she began painting landscapes and farm scenes from memory, producing more than 1,000 paintings. In 1939, three of her paintings were displayed at the Museum of Modern Art in New York City, launching her reputation.

◄ GRAFFITI ART

Keith Haring (1958-1990) started out as a New York subway graffiti artist. He is best known for his graffiti-style chalk figures surrounded by lines suggesting rapid movement. He popularized the production of quickly painted murals that he created with the help of inner-city youth.

WORK FOR CHILDREN ▲

An author and illustrator of children's books, Maurice Sendak was awarded the Caldecott Medal in 1964 for *Where the Wild Things Are*, a book that has sold more than 2.5 million copies. Many of Sendak's stories are inspired by Jewish folk tales, and many characters resemble his own relatives.

THE STAGE

In the early years of the 20th century, before the invention of movies, radio, and television, there were as many as 250 theatrical productions in one Broadway season! Today, Broadway offers some 25 productions a season. Theater continues to thrive all over the country, from Los Angeles to Chicago to New York to Houston to Atlanta.

VAUDEVILLE DAYS

At vaudeville's height in the 1920s, its variety shows—which featured acrobats, singers, comedians, jugglers, magicians, and trained animal acts—were seen by two million people a week! The Palace Theater in New York City was at the center of it all. Although vaudeville collapsed in the 1930s, many of its stars, such as W. C. Fields and the Marx Brothers (*right*), went on to success in movies.

Chico, Groucho, and Harpo (with scissors).

▲ ZIEGFELD'S FOLLIES

In the early 1900s, one of Broadway's most popular forms of entertainment was the musical revue: a variety show featuring singers, dancers, and a chorus of beautiful girls. Florenz Ziegfeld, producer of *Ziegfeld's Follies*, spared no expense for his productions. He boasted that his star, Anna Held, bathed in milk, and his chorus girls wore silk stockings.

WILL ◀ ROGERS

Will Rogers (1879-1935) began his career as a cowboy, but was soon well-known as a rope twirler and trick rider in Wild West shows. His sense of humor earned him a name in vaudeville as a political satirist from 1915 to 1924. He also wrote a column for *The New York Times*, and became a film star and radio personality.

A CHORUS LINE ▼
This Tony Award-winning musical ran for a record-breaking fifteen years, opening in 1975 and closing in 1990. Conceived, directed, and choreographed by Michael Bennett, A Chorus Line draws its story from a set of fictional characters gathered for auditions for a Broadway musical.

IT AIN'T NECESSARILY SO

THE THEATRE GUILD presents

PORGY and BESS
MUSIC BY
GEORGE GERSHWIN
LIBRETTO BY
DUBOSE HEYWARD
LYRICS BY
DUBOSE HEYWARD and IRA GERSHWIN
PRODUCTION DIRECTED BY ROUBEN MAMOULIAN

THE LION KING ▼
Disney's stage adaptation of its animated film The Lion King took Broadway by storm when it opened in November 1997. Winner of six Tony awards, including Best Musical, The Lion King showcases more than 100 puppets representing 25 kinds of animals, including life-size elephants with a human performer in each limb.

PORGY AND BESS
In 1935, George Gershwin composed Porgy and Bess, one of the first American operas. Gershwin took his inspiration from a love story set among poor African-Americans in Charleston. Audiences were stunned by its realistic portrayals and "stayed away in droves." Today, however, Porgy and Bess is hailed as a masterpiece.

13

LET'S DANCE!

A form of expression, dance can tell a story through music and movement instead of words. Dancing is also just plain fun entertainment.

Child star Shirley Temple sang and tap danced with Bill "Bojangles" Robinson in the movie *The Little Colonel* (1935).

▲ TA
MA
One of America's most famous dancer
and an inspiration to a generation of tap
pers, Gene Kelly (1912-1996) starred i
and codirected such film musicals a
Singin' in the Rain (1952

TIP! TAP!

When the Irish jig met the African juba, tap was born. In the 1920s and 30s, this new American dance form became popular with the movies and stage shows of Bill "Bojangles" Robinson (*above*). Tap's popularity continues today with the phenomenal Savion Glover, whose role in *Bring in Da Noise, Bring in Da Funk* brought the history of tap before audiences around the world.

DANCE ON AND ON ▼

In the worst days of the Great Depression, there was a craze for dance marathons. Unlike the marathons of today, which usually raise money for charitable causes, these were conducted for profit. Each couple paid to compete for a cash prize as they danced for weeks—even months!

LET'S TWIST

Chubby Checker's live performance of the Twist on Dick Clark's dance show *American Bandstand*, sent Americans twisting over dance floors everywhere. From 1960 to 1962, Checker's song "The Twist" was number one on the American pop music charts for 40 weeks!

GET DOWN TONIGHT!

During the disco era, which peaked in the 1970s, the movie *Saturday Night Fever*, starring John Travolta, popularized such dances as the Bump and the Bus Stop.

AILEY'S TROUPE ▲

Drawing inspiration from the body language of urban black America, Alvin Ailey (1931-1989) choreographed dances that have been seen by more than 19 million people in at least 70 countries. The Alvin Ailey American Dance Theatre—the first modern dance troupe to be completely multiracial—has a repertory of more than 190 works by more than 60 choreographers.

◄ TAKING A BREAK

Born on the streets of New York's Harlem and South Bronx, breakdancing evolved from youth gangs taking a break from fighting to compete with one another using acrobatic dance moves, such as the Moonwalk, the Robot, and the Electric Boogie.

SHOW OR SPORT

The great American appetite for displays of physical prowess has created new forms of entertainment, some of which have all the grace of ballet and the speed and skill of athletic events.

B-BALL BALLY-HOO

The Harlem Globetrotters are known for their spectacular ball-handling and unpredictable hijinks. Founded in 1927 as one of the first African-American professional teams, the Globetrotters have literally "trotted" the globe, breaking records for audience attendance. As player Meadowlark Lemon explained, "It's all about entertaining."

LET'S RODEO!

Rodeo (Spanish for "round up") has its roots in the 1800s, when cowboys from different ranches would compete to see who was the best at breaking wild horses, roping calves, and wrestling steers—the ordinary chores of ranching. Today, rodeos are big business. They attract thousands of fans and professional cowboys and cowgirls.

▲ TAKING A DIP

Visitors to Billy Rose's famous 1930s nightclub were drawn by an unusual floorshow: a huge pool full of swimming dancers. Since that time, synchronized swimming has made its mark as an art form and an Olympic event.

16

STUNTMAN ▼

Where there's little risk, there's little reward—so said the motorcycle daredevil Evel Knievel. His stunts were always bigger, better, and more dangerous than the last. In his most spectacular stunt, Knievel tried jumping Snake River Canyon in Idaho, but failed to make the leap when his parachutes deployed on take-off.

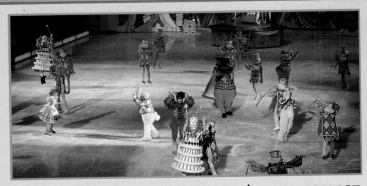

▲ SHOW ON ICE

The most elegant of winter sports and a popular event in the Winter Olympics since 1976, ice-dancing features deft jumps and spins. Skating partners demonstrate strength and agility as they move at tremendous speeds across the ice. Today, even theatrical dance shows are staged on ice.

▲ MACHINE MINDED

The tractor-pull event at county fairs has given way to a new form of machine jockeying that attracts thousands at exhibitions held across the nation. Monster truck shows feature 10,000-pound trucks that go from zero to 70 miles per hour in less than five seconds, fly through the air, do wheelies, and crawl over and crush rows of cars.

WRESTLING FOR REAL?

Both sport and show, professional wrestling attracts more than 30 million viewers in America, who tune to cable television's *Raw is War* or *Nitro* to see their favorite wrestlers piledrive, spear, stun, or smash their opponents in contests that are carefully planned and dramatically staged.

START UP THE MUSIC!

American music has come a long way since 1892, when John Phillip Sousa (*left*) founded his Sousa Band, an all-brass marching band. Sousa tunes were lively and loud, to "make a man with a wooden leg step out." Sousa composed more than 100 marches, including the Fourth of July favorite "The Stars and Stripes Forever."

▼ BOUND FOR GLORY

Woody Guthrie, a folk hero and political activist, sang about the sufferings of ordinary people during the Great Depression of the 1930s. Inspired by the old English ballads still sung by people in the Appalachian Mountains, Guthrie's work inspired the protest songs of the 1960s, and the folk-styled music of Bob Dylan and Joan Baez.

PIANO MAN

Pianist and composer Scott Joplin (1868-1917) was dubbed "the King of Ragtime Writers." Joplin combined his training in European classical music with African-American rhythms. His "Maple Leaf Rag," a huge hit, spread the bouncy, honky-tonk sound of ragtime across turn-of-the-century America.

PLAYIN' ▶ THE BLUES

Muddy Waters (1915-1984) combined the Delta blues of his native Mississippi with the sounds of his adopted city, Chicago. His style of singing and playing electric guitar influenced countless musicians—including the Rolling Stones, whose name comes from a Waters song.

18

Trumpet player Louis Armstrong (1900-1971) was a jazz pioneer. He invented "scat"—a style of singing using sounds instead of words.

Blues singer Billie Holiday (1915-1959), known as Lady Day, used her expressive, haunting voice to add emotional impact to popular songs.

HOT JAZZ

Jazz is a rhythmic music that features spur-of-the-moment solos. In the early 1900s, jazz was one of the attractions of the Cotton Club, Harlem's famous nightclub. At the Cotton Club, movie stars, gangsters, and political figures rubbed elbows as they listened to great jazz performers, such as Billie Holiday, Cab Calloway, and Duke Ellington.

◀ OL' BLUE EYES

The first teen idol to make listeners melt was Frank Sinatra (left). A "balladeer," or singer of romantic songs, "Ol' Blue Eyes" wowed them with his warm baritone. In the early 1940s, fan clubs of "bobby soxers" flourished across the country, and girls fainted and screamed at Sinatra's concerts.

SWINGING CATS

In 1934, clarinetist Benny Goodman and his "hot swing" band toured the country. Everywhere they went, they were greeted by young enthusiastic audiences eager to Jitterbug, Lindy Hop, and do the Big Apple. Soon other bandleaders, such as Tommy Dorsey, Glenn Miller (*in background*), and Count Basie, had formed "big bands," and big-band swing became the sound of the WWII era.

ALL-AMERICAN SOUNDS

The 20th century has seen the birth of many new American musical styles—including jazz, swing, rock 'n' roll, and rap—and some unforgettable music idols.

Pop idol Madonna created a sensation in the 1980s with her dance music and showy fashion statements. The term *wannabe* was coined for all the young people who wanted to be just like her.

R-E-S-P-E-C-T! ▼

Aretha Franklin earned her "Queen of Soul" title by thrilling audiences with her powerful voice. Daughter of a preacher, she grew up listening to and singing with gospel choirs—roots that give her R&B and soul hits their special sound.

▲ KING OF ROCK

Alan Freed was the first white disc jockey to play black R&B (rhythm and blues) records. The catchy tunes became so popular among young people, that white artists, such as Elvis Presley, began recording them in the 1950s. Presley ushered in rock 'n' roll, sending teens into a frenzy with his romantic voice, defiant sneer, and wild style of moving on stage.

FAN-TASTIC FAME ▲

Grateful Dead fans are the kind that most bands can only dream about! When the band tours, true "Deadheads" follow it, catching as many concerts as possible. The Dead are famous for their live concerts and laid-back rock style—as well as for their fans.

MAN ▶

WITH A MESSAGE

Bob Dylan's protest songs "Blowin' in the Wind" and "The Times They Are A-Changin'" became theme songs of the 1960s' civil-rights and antiwar movements. Dylan's music blends his main influences: country, blues, Woody Guthrie's thoughtful lyrics, and Elvis Presley's rock energy.

THE MOTOWN SOUND ▲

The famous "Motown sound" was created by Detroit songwriter and record producer Berry Gordy. Motown Records featured such talents as Stevie Wonder, Ray Charles, The Supremes, Marvin Gaye and the Jackson Five (*above*).

STREET RAP

Will Smith (*above*) and partner DJ Jazzy Jeff won the first-ever Grammy Award in the rap category. Rappers speak, chant, and sing their rhyming lyrics, called rap, to a repetitive rhythm called hip-hop. Rap is a kind of storytelling. It often features a social message, and describes rebellious and violent big-city lifestyles.

NEW COUNTRY ▲

When Garth Brooks began performing, his music reflected his idols, country stars George Strait and George Jones. But as Brooks's tastes expanded to include Billy Joel, KISS, Queen, and other rockers, his music changed. His chart-topping blend of country, rock, and pop gave new life to country music.

21

AMERICA'S EYE

Nearly 50 years ago, television sets replaced fireplaces as the gathering spots for families, and new audiences made the leap from listening to dramas and comedies on the radio to watching them on "the boob tube."

"MY NAME'S FRIDAY"

Dragnet, the most popular detective show of the 1950s, lured millions to their sets. It pioneered realism on the small screen. Producer, director, and star Jack Webb (*right*) combed police files for story ideas and re-created a Los Angeles police station—down to the original doorknobs—on the studio lot.

"TO THE MOON, ALICE!" ▲

Traffic cops noted fewer auto on the road wheneve *The Honeymooner* aired. Brooklyn bu driver Ralph Cramder (Jackie Gleason), hi long-suffering wife, Alice (Audrey Meadows), and goof neighbor Ed Norton (Art Carney drew 60 million viewers a week in the 1950s—and have been ham ming it up in reruns ever since

YOUR SHOW OF SHOWS

What a line-up! Funny-men Woody Allen, Mel Brooks, Carl Reiner, and Neil Simon got their start writing skits for *Your Show of Shows*. A kind of 1950s *Saturday Night Live*, this program made host Sid Caesar one of TV's first superstars.

MOUSE EARS ▲

"Who's the leader of the club that's made for you and me? M-I-C-K-E-Y M-O-U-S-E!" From 1955 to 1959, talented young Mouseketeers sang, danced, and introduced Disney cartoons every afternoon on *The Mickey Mouse Club*.

"GOOD NIGHT, JOHN-BOY." ▼

Sweetly sentimental, *The Waltons* centered on the struggles and joys of a big family in Depression-era Virginia. Narrated by John-Boy, the eldest son, it aired from 1972 to 1981, and spawned other family dramas, such as *Little House on the Prairie*.

WILD WESTERN ▼

Ben Cartwright and his sons may have squabbled, but they always united when outlaws or wild animals threatened their Nevada ranch! One of the first TV shows filmed in color, *Bonanza* aired for 14 years and drew some 400 million viewers—from African villagers to Buckingham Palace royals.

▲ THE ENTERPRISE

Thirty years, four TV series, and nine feature films later, *Star Trek* is as popular as ever. Created in 1966, the original *Star Trek* brought the crew of the *Starship Enterprise*, led by Captain James T. Kirk and first officer Mr. Spock, into strange galaxies of the 23rd century.

TV ALL THE TIME

More channels, more programs, more of the time—that's the slogan of today's TV networks. But as "the box" encounters its third generation of viewers, the ingredients for hits remain the same: drama, laughs, and just enough fascinating info to educate as well as entertain.

"DON'T HAVE A COW, MAN"

First broadcast in 1987 on *The Tracey Ullman Show*, the Simpsons have become America's favorite cartoon clan. Animator Matt Groening's bug-eyed Homer, blue-haired Marge, and bratty Bart raise sarcasm to a prime-time art, poking fun at popular movies, politics, and even themselves.

TEEN APPEAL

She's just your average high school student—or is she? Based on a popular comic book character, *Sabrina the Teenage Witch* conjures up the pains and pleasures of dating, the prom, and homework—with a few spells thrown in for laughs!

IN THE FORM OF A QUESTION

The answer: *Jeopardy*. The question: what's the number-one game show in America? Hosted by Alex Trebek, *Jeopardy* has given away $34 million over 30 years to contestants providing the correct questions for answers ranging from "Cheese" to *Charlie's Angels*.

YADA, YADA, YADA ▲

The *Seinfeld* sitcom attracted 30 million viewers with its plots about. . .well, nothing. A wild cast of atypical characters, and plots that showed the humor of everyday life, kept Jerry & friends on the air for nine seasons.

ALL ABOUT OPRAH ▼

Tackling a range of topics from bank-ruptcy to fat-free cooking, The Oprah Winfrey Show has changed the face of TV. Actress, producer, philanthropist, book-club sponsor, and self-help guru for 33 million viewers world-wide, Winfrey has become the first African-American and the third woman in history to head her own production company.

THE TRUTH IS OUT THERE ▼

It's dark, it's raining, and FBI agents Scully (Gillian Anderson) and Mulder (David Duchovny) are investigating the X-Files—dark government conspiracies, alien abductions, vampires, and any other eerie thing you can imagine. A lavishly produced series, The X-Files has won multiple awards and spawned novels and a feature film.

THE MUPPETS ▲

Puppeteer Jim Henson (1936-1990) created his first Muppet, Kermit the Frog, in 1955. Henson's performance on programs such as The Ed Sullivan Show attracted national attention. By 1969, the Muppets were featured on the children's program Sesame Street, and soon Oscar the Grouch, Bert and Ernie, and Big Bird became household names. Kermit the Frog went on to star in The Muppet Show, the most widely seen TV program in the world from 1976 to 1981.

THE FIRST FLICKERS

Early moviegoers went to arcades called nickelodeons to watch "flickers"—short, cheaply made films. When these early movies gave way to better productions in the 1920s, "picture palaces" were built in major cities across the U.S. New York City's Roxy Theater seated more than 6,200 people!

HAPLESS HERO

The Little Tramp, signature character of silent-film star Charlie Chaplin (1889-1977), is one of the most-recognized figures in all of film. Chaplin's hero made people laugh—and sometimes cry—as he suffered all sorts of indignities but never lost heart.

BEYOND LIVING COLOR

The first color films were handpainted with the aid of a microscope. It wasn't until 1932 that Technicolor film was invented. *The Wizard of Oz* (1939) (*above*) treated viewers to a vibrantly yellow brick road, brilliantly red ruby slippers, and a creepily green-faced Wicked Witch.

VAMPIRE MANIA

There have been more than 150 movie versions of *Dracula*, which makes it the most film-popular subject of all time! Based on Bram Stoker's novel, the most famous *Dracula*, released in 1931, starred Bela Lugosi (*above*) as the 500-year-old Transylvanian.

LOVE THAT MOUSE!

Walt Disney's fun-loving Mickey Mouse became a star in *Steamboat Willie* in 1928, but it was a fairy-tale heroine who starred in Disney's first long-playing cartoon feature in 1937. Called "Disney's folly" because it cost $1.5 million to make, *Snow White and the Seven Dwarfs* eventually made back its investment and became the most popular cartoon ever made.

HAIRY APE

Some spectacular—for 1933—effects went into making *King Kong*, the story of a monster ape that terrorizes New York. Kong was actually a 24-inch model made of jointed metal and covered in rabbit fur.

TRAILBLAZER ▲

Stagecoach (1939), starring John Wayne, lifted American Westerns out of a mass of one-dimensional adventure films and into drama that worked on many levels. The film's nine characters faced dangers that thrilled audiences, but also made them think about social ills and human nature.

SHAKING THINGS UP ▲

Movie audiences of the 1950s were used to clean-cut, happy-looking teenagers—then *The Wild One* (1954) roared into town! Young Marlon Brando played the moody, rebellious leader of a motorcycle gang, complete with leather jacket, jeans, and a scowl.

MOVIE MAGIC

Many of today's biggest hit movies feature high-tech effects that play as important a part in the film as the actors or sets. In fact, these inventions sometimes create virtual sets, ones that exist on the screen rather than in the studio.

TITANIC TECHNOLOGY

When you look at the thousands of passengers strolling the deck in the movie *Titanic*, you're not seeing just a picture filmed by a camera—you're also seeing hundreds of gigabytes of data. To create the blockbuster visual effects of the sinking ship, 200 computer terminals worked 24 hours a day for 2 months, processing 800 million computer instructions per second!

MORPHING

A computer technique called morphing, in which the pixels of a scanned image are made to blend into another image, was used to create the dazzling special effects in the 1994 Jim Carrey comedy *The Mask*.

STAR WARS

Featuring film's all-time evil character, Darth Vader—and his Evil Empire—*Star Wars* put audiences on the edge of their seats. Filming the space chases in *Star Wars* required "motion control," a special technique in which model spaceships stay still while the camera moves on rails towards them, filming them against a blue background. Finally, an optical computer printer assembles all the shots against a background of stars, making a single film sequence of amazing reality.

IS IT REAL?

Most of the lifelike dinosaurs in *Jurassic Park* (1993) were generated by 3-D computer scanners. Actors did their parts before a blue screen. Then photographed images were scanned and converted by computer into thousands of small image points called pixels, which can be played with to create amazing effects.

ORIGINAL ART

Computer technology assisted with some remarkable sequences in *The Lion King*, including a stampede in which a herd of wildebeests flows past the camera's eye. But computers cannot do everything—this Disney original was created by nearly 400 artists, who used live animals for models.

THE BIG SCREEN

Movie-going is at its best when a theater has a big screen. IMAX produces pictures three times the standard wide-screen size, while Omnimax uses special lenses to cast spectacular images on to curved domes above the audience's heads. Some IMAX movies are in 3-D, which require the audience to wear 3-D glasses (*above, background*). The experience causes viewers to duck and dodge trains, elephants, and other things that seem to be jumping off the big screen.